THE BEES
HAVE BEEN
CANCELED

✿

THE BEES
HAVE BEEN
CANCELED

❊

MAYA
CATHERINE
POPA

NEW MICHIGAN PRESS
TUCSON, ARIZONA

NEW MICHIGAN PRESS

DEPT OF ENGLISH, P. O. BOX 210067

UNIVERSITY OF ARIZONA

TUCSON, AZ 85721-0067

<http://newmichiganpress.com>

Orders and queries to <nmp@thediagram.com>.

ISBN 978-1-934832-59-2. FIRST PRINTING.

Printed in the United States of America.

Design by Ander Monson.

Cover image courtesy of Lourdes Sanchez and
Sears-Peyton Gallery.

CONTENTS

THE BEES HAVE BEEN CANCELED

Never again the humming, saddled flowers. Never the blind oath by a velveteen prisoner. Never the yellow, hula hooped in black, little engine left running late into the darkness. Oh, how they were charming, clever monographs. Sunlight couldn't save them from the angel of extinction. Virgil said they swell with nectar's tilted knowledge. I don't know what to believe. Maybe they tired of being addicts. Clover honey, garbage honey, accidental ice cream honey. Ransomed stamen, sweetsinful will-do-anything-for honey. Maybe they caught fevers at midnight with no one there to hold their stingers, no fat queen to press a cold compress. How will we currency honey from wildflowers, that liquid of languages? How pollinate in the bees' electrostatic absence? How will the bellbirds take it, the Canterbury birds? Who will cast the last skeleton in amber? I'll miss the noise, the palimpsestic clamor, soft shock of discovering a hive under your roof. The lull as each integer walked its body over a blossom, then flew away with its instructions.

URANIUM IN ENGLISH

1.

A nuclear death shares
its colors with the parrotfish—

chainslick, moccasin,
ice breaker, gigawatt.

The Alabama Shot
stocks "My First Rifles,"

guns in a variety of colors,
pink for girls to shoot squirrels.

I'm arranging information
available to anyone.

2.

I teach my class
the problem/solution structure.

Many logical questions are asked,
several logical solutions proposed.

What about the squirrels?
I ask my students.

Whole neighborhoods
annihilated in Hiroshima,

classrooms like cartoon
shadows in Nagasaki.

We agree one violence
is greater than the others,

but a string of tiny violences
makes the largest possible.

3.

A boy with a cricket rifle
kills his sister in Kentucky.

No teacher can show him
how to live with it,

no diagram of the body,
no pull-down map

can illustrate the wound
spread across his days.

Not Latin odes, not physics—
his parents can't teach him,

nor his other siblings;
not the man who sold

his father this miniature
with the knowledge

he'd outgrow it
like a pair of shoes.

4.

In 1789, uranium is found
asleep aside anonymous metals.

The bullet, one could say,
was always inside of us,

the club a casual
extension of our arms.

And if all of our limitations
are armed, what's left

to keep a citizen clean,
what glove can fit

our knuckle's trigger?

5.

And don't imagine
it gets easier hearing about it,

I tell my students, or do I,
when they mention

the errant shooting,
nuclear test, and I worry

for the seasons which cannot
worry for each other,

summer like a fog that won't
dissolve, the end of snow.

Too late to worry, says Jorie;
I do not tell them this.

Instead I say: what color
is a disagreement between

friends, between nations—
what does being right look like?

And the shame is that the parrotfish
cannot be remade from scratch,

while the delicate,
collectible uranium glass

will glow into infinity,
a Vaseline sheen.

THE GOVERNMENT HAS BEEN CANCELED

& my friend has just dissected a body in medical school,
of which we have not spoken, knowing there are privacies

we must pretend are still intact.   The panda cam is off:
    people are distressed

that someone will forget to feed the cub
unless the live-feed's breathing in the toolbar. I spend the
    afternoon

dreaming a rebellion I could stage
                and still show up to my body the next morning,

        life the way it was promised
on sitcoms where everyone gets to be alive for 20 minutes
        not worrying about the debt ceiling or health insurance.

My friend makes the first of many incisions
into that cold familiar otherness.

I turn to obituaries for proof
that people still matter to one another
        in towns where stores bear the names of the deceased.

Today, the Library of Congress is canceled

which makes it difficult to do my job,
checking dates of publications and answering questions
    such as "are preachers and reverends interchangeable in
    most faiths."

From this description, it is impossible to say what I do.

                I go home burdened & amplified by knowledge,
        live in the world this information refers to—
    there is no better, other way to do this.

The government is canceled
but not the body: not the bodies furloughed
            not the bodies waiting

                    for my friend to break them tenderly.

MEDITATION HAVING FELT AND FORGOTTEN

after Robert Hass

All the new thinking is about preempting feeling.
In this way, it is incompatible with all the old thinking
but easier to stomach. For instance,
how birds land on water without closing their eyes
doesn't remind me how I sought you with an appetite
more pressing than fear. And the year our passion took—
how flat to call it lust, how wrong to call its mimicry love
when little love was made with which to mistake it.

All the new thinking is about straightening the facts.
Your hands disappeared, water drying over weeks.
I learned that pain's the lack of place to point to.
Would have made the trade: me for you, us for anything.
Would have said anything over and over, *blackberry*,
dance party, silverfish like Typhon imitating voices.
What an unfair tax on time desire is,
a year of spell-work to break that staring contest.

All the new thinking is about drugging up
to let go of the mark desire leaves on the body.
The new thinking's about saying goodbye to the body
flamed into a maddening nothing. You didn't even die—
was that the problem? Hardly to do with her
or with him. Sometimes I set aside the afternoon
to relive what feels like caricature: walks under
the George Washington Bridge, neither of us knowing

to enjoy the company. Time's passed, yes,
left me a diamond of bitterness; I see the water brace
itself for my reflection, circle the stitch where absence
dropped its anchor—but I'm alive and capable
of meditation. Walking through chokecherry trees,
language seems accomplice to grieving, everything
dissolves to make words possible: joy sours,
brevity distends, silence tows its dragline to the finish.

Poem, close your palm: you ask nothing in return.
Think how far you've come through afternoons and evenings
when loss seemed to whistle from the manholes,
your hands staining everything with blackberry blood.

THE MASTER'S PIECES

Iron violet, slingshot carnation, who doesn't envy the painter's
    do-overs,
doesn't dream of white's division, colors spun into a stupor.

The more I write, the leaner the binary. Two colors, one ascent
over twenty-six stepladders.

Who doesn't envy the painter's process, bodies kneaded out of light
into cool uninjured nothingness.

A painter knows her subject when she sees it, figure all flood,
all inside-out wolf, as immediate a hook as any hitch in logic.

Writing seems absurd by comparison. My hands listen to my
    brain listens
to my listening. Black on flagstone, bodiless cursive

I write out and back in, and if I'm a master at anything, it's taking out
the names till something

reveals itself. The pleasure of a landscape is immediate:
there forever and by addition you all of a sudden, suddenly
    there's you

by the haystacks holding a bridle. Or is that the writer again
fawning on a feeling, dreaming of wool's division into further wool,

hoping to halve and to have and examine closely,
too closely, and still, to keep on having.

Every poem has something trying to escape
by a tear the length of its idiom. A name that can be vanquished

by anaphora (who doesn't envy that?). Then suddenly there's a
    you again
as per our lore. As per our lore, the sky tries to tell me
    something.

I look till there's no distance between me and the looking.

THE SEER DREAMS ANTIGONE

It is not advised to weep for the children of your enemies,
    though if you do it in the privacy
        of your home,   who can judge you?

And no one can tell you the order of action
is for the greater good
    if little seems in order, if even less
                seems good.

        Oh, night is a compelling orator,
      the jasmines flicker on and off.

When your enemy sees your fig trees,
he will be reminded of his son's uneven hair,
    but in your brother he will find
only a poor imitation.

Do not let anyone catch you burying the body.

        Hide his body in your own
      until the lights go out,
then pray for negligence, black sails
    left unchanged,
              dull spot in the electric fence.

    If you do not speak up for the body,
      the wrong person will speak for it.

Numberless labors await
an emptied will.
                        And who can say
if the mind is worse than what's out there
                        circling the night.

WANDMAKER

Again I am thinking of the wandmaker,
his labor equal parts language and device,
whittling the wood, polishing a word.

How things must sometimes end up
in the wrong hands for history to happen.
Every bomb and every bomb maker

has a signature. Even the anchor
reading from a teleprompter
is surprised by what he has just had to say

and explains its the particular bouquet
of shrapnel, breed of agony that marks
the maker. I try, but there's no way

to sleep off this violence. I spin in place
under a rainbow parachute pulled tight
by my kindergarten classmates.

Any one could be a runner in Boston.
The anchor reads the names of two
brothers, and I look for signs of certain

evil. Are these my people, my misguided
people, and how should I keep on
loving them, forgiving them, who can

teach you that, really? Everything
gets languaged eventually, even silence
flourishes rhetorically—*that's all for now*

folks, stay tuned. The wandmaker tunes
the wood then steps aside for utterance
to draw a shape in the sacrificial air.

YARD SALE

Books, aromatherapy kits, and sheet music—
objects that have lived in the presence of people
and will need new owners to remain relevant.
The cups would like to be adopted as a set,
the spaghetti measurer is skittish around children.
Someone has left a newspaper balancing
between two levels of a tiered table. The front page
glitters with bad news, anything good
is tucked into metaphor: a rollercoaster of
emotions later, the dog returns unharmed
and the family resumes its battles against
the perils on page 1. No one wants to buy anything.
They want to peer into each other's lives,
press their mouths to strangers' cups
and lift affinities, a few words of Swedish,
a talent for Sudoku. I lay the news by the music
and patchouli to see if that will unbully it.
Someone organizes hurt by color, the blue table
dark as the underbelly of an avalanche.
There I place an orange napkin, copy of Keats,
and hope for a handover of idle goodness,
a share of warmth stored in our sugars
passed through the vellum of our touch.
Home, an ant drowns in my espresso.
I hold a vigil; I can still hear the voice of my teacher
reading the part of the ant in a picture book.

We're counted on to make a safety of our minds,
a world out of objects shared between us.
I kiss the cup held by my two hands.
My mouth might mend a stranger's mouth.

THE COLOR WHEEL HAS BEEN CANCELED

Color spoils us, palette for each season: it's a shame for other, paler senses. I can hardly smell an argument between two stars, what a murder the night sky is behind clouds. Color echoes in every open eye, even when you'd like to be unaccompanied. Wolves and birches in a tender binary. Only milk and snow are truly white, the rest scurries from birth to blight on the color wheel. Brides tarnish, calcium chips, the ermine only occasionally visits. The diver can never unsee a coral, nor the lover the lover.

He gave me a moon garden, bouquet of truces on thin stems.
    I was a hurricane, gutted and spun by my own hunger.
My mouth bred cavities, mouthfuls of argentine.

Never a sorer white than when I spoke. And spoken to,
    I was a moon garden, earth and ether,
altered by my distances.

Sun fattens, bends over earth like a resistance band. Water glows, grows frugal with moonlight. Manta rays glide like unfinished angels swallowing a cameraman's spotlight.

IS THIS YOUR BAG PLEASE WOULD YOU OPEN IT

The moment you know they are about to find something
pushing aside the mini marmalades
withdrawing the curler with latex fingers
folding a flap   folding back   another flap
your underwear grinning   not getting the situation
placed inside a box   PROPERTY OF HEATHROW:
it isn't personal   though it sure feels
like it's personal   when a man asks you
how long you spent in Romania   when moments ago
you said you were in London   and packed your own
bag   who else would pack your fucking bag

but he thinks it's charming
to get things wrong   or maybe professional
to run on a hunch   he swipes the straps
for a bomb test   banters while your bras
feel badly for you   they never wanted this   in spite
of their lace finally he finds the toiletries case   delays
the pleasure of admonishing you   for Alice-sized lotions
stolen from hotels   into another box they go
it's a job   remember   you can't take it personally
if he hands you his number on a food court receipt
                        …prettiest terrorist I've seen all day…
is this your privacy   and can he keep it?

SASHIMI

I served my loves' sashimi hearts
on iceless beds of clean bamboo.
Some were tasteless, others,
spoiled at the oil-rig of our departure.
There was the horse-mackerel
bucking at the rice, as if another life
were to await. The wheel-shrimp
hugging his white station like a pillow,
the koi promising to love each grain.
I knew the knife-work it had taken
to get here, the hands, my hands,
unfolding origami nerves, widening
fields between modest fish lungs.
I could smell blood on the stone floor,
heard a bell that signaled the start
of an auction. I plucked and plucked
at another urchin's stitches
as my own heart shivered on the scale.

PALIMPSEST

Flower-bordered river
where I fillet the hyacinths,

a Russian doll of places
posing as one place.

Halogen me
at a horse show in Florida

while another juliennes
olives for appetizers.

A doll slipped in another
till all dolls are dull:

versions of me
with whistles for lips

reciting asterisks
in the periodic table.

Collage of the unconscious:
white flowers, lost teeth,

scarecrow with
an aureole of straw,

basilica for everyone's
best dresses.

I visit the public
museum of clouds,

lithographs of sky
posing as space.

Layers make monsters
as shows the snapdragon.

Memory, you crooked thing
I do to the page.

THE END OF THE WORLD HAS BEEN CANCELED

Pygmalion of anonymous days
glossed, fitted for the reckoning ball.

*

Dawn parts trawler fish,
lustrous deaths
on Seaport's docks.

*

What's the difference between
periphery & prophecy?

The end's a fence
deactivated at night.

*

I threaten the mailman with empty packages,
tell him I can smell greetings on his fingers,

the carmine ink & cadence of proposals
composed just under the wire.

*

What do we know of this tilting life,
fresh out of Babel & into outer space?

The fluency of arches, driftwood
of truces, light the rift between

tomorrow, no tomorrow,

two movies competing
for the same ticket.

EAGLE

Today's violence is cross-referenced
under technology.

An eagle shot in the face by a hunter
successfully receives

a replacement beak. I do not know
who these people are

who snipe the sky & walk off
when they know they've missed the heart.

I know the eyes that spot
the dying animal, abandoned

for what's called nature to deal with.
The hands responsible

for lifting the face & deciding to undo
what another human has done to it.

Someone will have to stabilize the bird
reading its deformity

for signs of infections.
Someone will have to see over

& over to suture the gash
where its beak once was,

another, engineer the yellow arc
so the bird can be outfitted

with a second chance,
photographed for science, released back

into its world as if only just returning
from a day hunting mice.

I wonder what the hunters think
of these efforts taken to undo

their recklessness, the delicate building
back to square one after a failed

annihilation, & whether the part
of the body that registers shame

is ever called upon to answer.

THE SONG OF MALE AGGRESSION

Singing is one of the most common ways
birds advertise that a territory belongs to them.

A boy offered me a necklace,
another cut it from my throat.
I'd forgotten until I heard the singing:
two robins in autumn disputing
open space. Once, I waited
without knowing for a nest
I could build in the dell of a voice.
Words for wanting bloomed in midair;
I learned to listen for variations.
What's not love in those words
finds others. But body, I was never
a bird leaving branches overhead
in case a dust hawk descends.
These men migrating from restlessness
to fatherhood, these birds perched
near the marrow of all memories
belong to me still, winding blue
through bowered nests. Sixteen,
we were always singing, were targets
ushered by longing and lament.
We split the silence and mended it.

THE RETURN TO NATURE HAS BEEN CANCELED

I used to think, if things got bad enough,
I could return to nature, its bell-less door ajar.

But after living selfishly for so long, it was difficult
adjusting to a new set of house rules. The rain

outnumbered us, the snow's word was final,
and soon, nature grew tyrannical, tubercular magnolias,

extended lives of fruit flies. I missed the microwave's
electric coronas, draining a power bar to its last interval.

Men rushed to marry earthquakes. The frost
used my body as its workbench. Wind drew echoes

from every hunter's ear. *Come here*, the deer called
and speared them, getting even. I asked a historian

to peruse the index for what could happen next.
No one could focus on "the course of action,"

first a man with a megaphone, then a girl
with nothing but the wind tunnel of her palm.

MINE'S NOT A POLITICAL HEART

All of my childhood fantasies—icescapes
with Alaskan cranes, treasure-diving
in the Black Sea—Putin has beat me to them.

He drapes a medal over his shadow
then extradites the dead from purgatory.
I live with this deadweight of humor

and scorn until the humor burns out.
I know my birthmarks aren't heraldic,
the sunspots transcribed don't form

a line of sheet music. Blinking, I kill
a group of gnats, *I kill only to see clearly.*
Give me refuge from that sentence,

freedom from the choir sanctioning.
Each day the grail looks more like a chalice,
each day, the chalice more like a mug.

ACKNOWLEDGMENTS

Day One: "The Song of Male Aggression"

Event Horizon: "Uranium in English"

FIELD: "The End of the World Has Been Canceled"

The Literary Review: "The Color Wheel Has Been Canceled"

The Los Angeles Review: "Is This Your Bag Please Would You Open It"

Narrative: "Yard Sale," "The Master's Pieces," "The Return to Nature Has Been Canceled," and "Meditation Having Felt and Forgotten"

The Paris-American: "Wandmaker"

Prelude: "Eagle" and "The Seer Dreams Antigone"

Southword Journal: "The Bees Have Been Canceled" and "Sashimi"

Tin House: "The Government Has Been Canceled" and "Mine's Not a Political Heart"